BASEBALL LEGENDS

Hank Aaron
Grover Cleveland Alexander
Ernie Banks
Johnny Bench
Yogi Berra
Roy Campanella
Roberto Clemente
Ty Cobb
Dizzy Dean
Joe DiMaggio
Bob Feller
Jimmie Foxx
Lou Gehrig
Bob Gibson
Rogers Hornsby
Reggie Jackson
Walter Johnson
Sandy Koufax
Mickey Mantle
Christy Mathewson
Willie Mays
Stan Musial
Satchel Paige
Brooks Robinson
Frank Robinson
Jackie Robinson
Babe Ruth
Tom Seaver
Duke Snider
Willie Stargell
Honus Wagner
Ted Williams
Carl Yastrzemski
Cy Young

JOHNNY BENCH

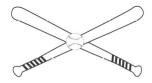

Mike Shannon

Introduction by
Jim Murray

Senior Consultant
Earl Weaver

CHELSEA HOUSE PUBLISHERS
New York • Philadelphia

Published by arrangement with
Chelsea House Publishers.
Newfield Publications is a federally
registered trademark of Newfield
Publications, Inc.

Produced by James Charlton Associates
New York, New York.

Designed by Hudson Studio
Ossining, New York.

Typesetting by LinoGraphics
New York, New York.

Picture research by Jennie McGregor
Cover illustration by Dan O'Leary

Library of Congress Cataloging-in-Publication Data

Shannon, Mike.
    Johnny Bench / Mike Shannon : introduction by Jim Murray.
    P. cm.—(Baseball legends)
    Includes bibliographical references (p.)
    Summary: A biography of the outstanding catcher who led the
Cincinnati Reds to four National League pennants and two World
Series victories in the 1970s.
            ISBN 0-7910-1168-2.—ISBN 0-7910-1202-6 (pbk.)
            1. Bench, Johnny. 1947- —Juvenile literature. 2. Baseball
players—United States—Biography—Juvenile literature. [1. Bench,
Johnny. 1947- . 2. Baseball players.] I. Title. II. Series.
        GV865.B35S53 1990
        92—dc20
        [796.357'092]
        [B]
                                90-31314
                                CIP
                                AC

CONTENTS

WHAT MAKES A STAR

Jim Murray

No one has ever been able to explain to me the mysterious alchemy that makes one man a .350 hitter and another player, more or less identical in physical makeup, hard put to hit .200. You look at an Al Kaline, who played with the Detroit Tigers from 1953 to 1974. He was pale, stringy, almost poetic-looking. He always seemed to be struggling against a bad case of mononucleosis. But with a bat in his hands, he was King Kong. During his career, he hit 399 home runs, rapped out 3,007 hits, and compiled a .297 batting average.

Form isn't the reason. The first time anybody saw Roberto Clemente step into the batter's box for the Pittsburgh Pirates, the best guess was that Clemente would be back in Double A ball in a week. He had one foot in the bucket and held his bat at an awkward angle—he looked as though he couldn't hit an outside pitch. A lot of other ballplayers may have had a better-looking stance. Yet they never led the National League in hitting in four different years, the way Clemente did.

Not every ballplayer is born with the ability to hit a curveball. Nor is exceptional hand-eye coordination the key to heavy hitting. Big-league locker rooms are filled with players who have all the attributes, save one: discipline. Every baseball man can tell you a story about a pitcher who throws a ball faster than anyone has ever seen but who has no control on or *off* the field.

The Hall of Fame is full of people who transformed themselves into great ballplayers by working at the sport, by studying the game, and making sacrifices. They're overachievers—and winners. If you want to find them, just watch the World Series. Or simply read about New York Yankee great Lou Gehrig; Ted Williams, "the Splendid Splinter" of the Boston Red Sox; or the Dodgers' strikeout king Sandy Koufax.

A pitcher *should* be able to win a lot of ballgames with a 98-miles-per-hour fastball. But what about the pitcher who wins 20 games a year with a fastball so slow that you can catch it with your teeth? Bob Feller of the Cleveland Indians got into the Hall of Fame with a blazing fastball that glowed in the dark. National League star Grover Cleveland Alexander got there with a pitch that took considerably longer to reach the plate; but when it did arrive, the pitch was exactly where Alexander wanted it to be—and the last place the batter expected it to be.

There are probably more players with exceptional ability who didn't make it to the major leagues than there are who did. A number of great hitters, bored with fielding practice, had to be dropped from their team because their home-run production didn't make up for their lapses in the field. And then there are players like Brooks Robinson of the Baltimore Orioles, who made himself into a human vacuum cleaner at third base because he knew that working hard to become an expert fielder would win him a job in the big leagues.

A star is not something that flashes through the sky. That's a comet. Or a meteor. A star is something you can steer ships by. It stays in place and gives off a steady glow; it is fixed, permanent. A star works at being a star.

And that's how you tell a star in baseball. He shows up night after night and takes pride in how brightly he shines. He's Willie Mays running so hard his hat keeps falling off; Ty Cobb sliding to stretch a single into a double; Lou Gehrig, after being fooled in his first two at-bats, belting the next pitch off the light tower because he's taken the time to study the pitcher. Stars never take themselves for granted. That's why they're stars.

1

A FITTING FAREWELL

On September 17, 1983, a record crowd of 53,790 fans packed into Cincinnati's Riverfront Stadium—not to watch a meaningless game between the last-place Reds and the third-place Houston Astros but to be on hand for Johnny Bench Night. Everyone wanted to say good-bye to the great Reds catcher, who would be retiring after the season.

It was late afternoon, but the sun still brightly lit the field. Banners, usually prohibited by the conservative Reds' management, hung from railings all around the stadium. One banner, which said, "Thanks for the Memories," seemed to express the widespread sentiment. Down on the field a rectangular red stage sat between the pitcher's mound and second base. Positioned in the center of the stage was Bench's chair. A red carpet stretching from a door in the right-center field wall to the infield indicated the path he would take to reach the platform. As soon as

Paul Householder and Nick Esasky greet a happy Bench after his home run on "Bench Night."

Bench stepped through the door in the outfield wall to officially begin Johnny Bench Night, the fans stood and gave him a tremendous ovation, which lasted several minutes. Bench walked slowly down the red carpet, often pausing along the way. As he progressed, he turned towards a different part of the stadium as if to establish a personal contact with each fan who had come out that night. Johnny waved his cap and blew giant kisses to the crowd as he slowly climbed the platform. Then he took a low dramatic bow.

When the applause died down, Johnny took a seat and the emcees introduced family members, teammates, the scout who had signed Bench, his best friend from high school, and others who had been important in Johnny's life. Then Bench was presented with a number of gifts, including: a wheelbarrow full of golf balls,one for each of Bench's career home runs, a fishing boat, a sterling silver plate designed with Bench's number 5 made of rubies, a golfing trip to Scotland, and a new Ford Bronco.

When the gift giving was over, it was time for Bench to speak to the crowd. He didn't talk long, but he spoke from the heart.

"Thanks to my friends for taking the time to be here. I am here because I love you. I chose to stay in Cincinnati for one reason; I love the city. I love the fans, and I was fortunate to play for the Reds. It has been a labor of love. I've tried to be the best player I could be, and it was easier because you were in back of me. I am very lucky, honored and grateful...I am going to try like hell to play good for you tonight."

The fans cheered even louder when the speech was over. But no one realized the best was yet to come.

In the first inning, the Astros' rookie pitcher Mike Madden walked Bench, and disappointed fans filled the stadium with boos. As Bench came to bat again in the third, the Reds were trailing 2-0 but had a runner on first with one out. This time Madden's control was better. On an 0-1 count he threw a fastball over the plate, and Bench took a vicious swing at it.

There was a sharp crack, and the ball sped on a line toward the left-field wall. The fans knew it was gone, and they went wild. It was the 389th home run of Bench's career, and it seemed as if he had propelled the ball over the wall through sheer will power just to give the fans a fitting farewell. It was to be his last home-run clout of his stellar career. And afterwards, he called the evening "the greatest night of my life." It was a storybook ending to a storybook career.

Bench waves to fans at the evening's tribute to him on September 17, 1983.

2

A BASEBALL BOYHOOD

Cincinnati manager Dave Bristol greets Johnny Bench at the spring training camp in 1969. Bristol was fired after the Reds finished in third place during the season.

The story started on December 7, 1947, when Johnny Lee Bench was born to Ted and Katy Bench in Oklahoma City, Oklahoma. The Benches already had two sons, Ted Jr., and William, and 19 months later their last child, Marilyn, would be born.

As a young man, Johnny's dad had dreamed of becoming a professional catcher, but he never made it to the big leagues. Ted Bench had high hopes for his sons, however, and he started teaching them the game as soon as they could walk. When Johnny's second-grade teacher asked the class what they wanted to be when they grew up, Johnny said he was going to be a professional baseball player. Everybody laughed, but Johnny was not kidding.

When Johnny was about five years old, the Bench family moved to the small town of Binger, Oklahoma. Two years later, Ted Bench started a Little League team called the Binger Bobcats. He made Johnny the team catcher because he

There was just one stop sign in Johnny's home-town of Binger, Oklahoma.

believed that becoming a good catcher was the quickest way to get to the majors.

As a boy, Johnny had unusually large hands and feet. His friends teased him about them, but his dad assured him he was built just right for a catcher. "Don't worry," Ted Bench said. "You'll grow into them."

Right from the beginning, young Bench had a good arm for the catching position, and his dad constantly worked with him to make it even better. During their many practice drills, Ted Bench moved second base twice the normal distance from home plate, a strategy that made Johnny's throws to second during regular games seem short and easy in comparison.

In the eighth grade, Johnny again announced that he was going to be a pro baseball player, and again the whole class laughed. But Johnny was so certain he would become a big leaguer that he worried when he got a C in penmanship. He did not want to be signing autographs with bad handwriting, so he spent hours at a time

Photography from the Lens of George Kalinsky

practicing his signature.

At the age of 14, Johnny began to play American Legion baseball with and against boys who were two, three, and even four year older than he. Nevertheless, he excelled, batting .355 his first year and over .400 his second.

With his American Legion team, as well as the Binger High School team, Johnny occasionally played first and third base. And because his arm was so strong, he often pitched. In addition to an 85 m.p.h. fastball, he had a sharp-breaking curveball and good control. He threw a no-hitter in American Legion ball, and his combined Legion–high school pitching record was an eye-opening 84-3.

Despite Johnny's impressive pitching, pro scouts were convinced that his future was behind the plate. They felt that as a catcher he had a powerful arm, and his ability as a hitter was just as spectacular. While still in high school, he hit a 400-foot home run, and one season he averaged .675. Johnny's future looked very bright; his potential, unlimited. Nobody was laughing any more at his desire to play major-league baseball.

But Johnny Bench almost did not make it to the majors. In fact, as the result of a tragic accident, he almost did not make it at all.

On April 1, 1965, during Johnny's senior year, the Binger High School baseball team was returning home after a game when the bus's brakes gave out going downhill.

Just before the bus hit a guard rail and flipped over, Johnny remembered what his dad, a professional truck driver, had told him to do if he ever found himself in such a situation: Get down on the floor! Johnny immediately pushed the boy sitting next to him to the floor, fell on top of him, and desperately grabbed onto the bottom of the seat.

The bus tumbled down a 50-foot incline into a ravine, flipping over twice more and tossing its helpless occupants around. Several boys were thrown out of the windows, and two of them were killed. But thanks to Johnny's quick thinking, both he and his seatmate escaped serious injury.

Despite his boyhood dreams of major-league stardom, Johnny had more than one option as he thought about his future. He was not only a super athlete, he was an excellent student. The valedictorian of his graduating class at Binger High, he received generous basketball and baseball scholarship offers from several colleges. Meanwhile, the Cincinnati Reds, who chose him after Bernie Carbo in the 1965 amateur draft, wanted to sign him for a bonus of only $5,000. Ted Bench felt the Reds' offer was too low and advised his son not to accept it.

For a while it seemed the Reds just might lose Johnny, who actually signed a letter of intent to play baseball for Phillips University in Enid, Oklahoma. But then the Reds upped their offer to $6,000 plus $8,000 tuition should Johnny decide to attend college later. Ted Bench still was not very impressed, but he left the decision up to his son. It did not take Johnny long to make up his mind: "I grew up to play baseball," he said. "That's what I'm going to do." And on June 21, 1965, 17-year-old Johnny Bench's dream came true. He became a member of the Cincinnati Reds organization.

Bench's pro career got off to a fast start when the manager of the Reds' Tampa, Florida, farm team put him into the game the very same night he arrived in town. Just a few hours later Johnny Bench was named the Tarpons' first-string catcher.

That night some of Johnny's new teammates

Johnny's picture in his high school year book is shown in a glass case in the school.

Photography from the Lens of George Kalinsky

let him sleep on the couch in their apartment. The next morning when he woke up and looked around at the unfamiliar surroundings, he felt scared. He wondered what in the world he was doing there. For the first time in his life, Johnny Bench was away from home, among virtual strangers, and completely on his own.

Johnny realized that he had to grow up fast. He knew that he was in a man's game, drawing a man's salary, and that it was no place for a boy. He realized there was no reason why he should not do his job.

A visit from his mom and dad helped Johnny overcome his homesickness, and then he got down to the business of playing ball. Once he got used to being on his own, his main concern was catching and hitting the Class A pitching of the Florida State League. He batted only .248 with two home runs and 35 RBI's in his first 68 games, but that was good enough to convince Johnny that he was definitely where he belonged.

But Johnny would not be there long. The Reds had big plans for him. That winter he played on their Instructional League team in Tampa along with the organization's other top prospects. One of the weekly news reports about the team plainly stated that the next Reds catcher would be Johnny Bench.

Bench began his second pro season with the Peninsula Grays of Newport News, Virginia, in the double A Carolina League and immediately ran into trouble against the tougher competition. He became frustrated and developed the bad habit of throwing his equipment in anger. One day he slammed his bat down so hard it cracked, and a piece of the bat flew up and stuck

Although Bench played fewer than one hundred games with the Peninsula Grays, his number was retired by the team.

in his neck. The Peninsula manager chewed Johnny out for that, and the accident, which could have been much worse, taught him to control his temper.

When Johnny finally settled down, he began tearing up the league. In one nine-game stretch he hit 9 home runs, and in 98 games he knocked out 22 homers and 68 RBI's. Bench's spectacular play took him to the league's All-Star game, where he threw out three runners in one inning. Before the season ended, he was promoted to the Bisons, the Reds' AAA team in Buffalo, New York.

Although he had not played there a full season, the Carolina League named Bench its Player of the Year. Just before he left for Buffalo the Grays retired his jersey number, the first

Cincinnati had four .300
hitters when this photo
was taken in late August of
1969. Bench tailed off to
.293 but Pete Rose led the
league with a .348
average. Shown here are
(left to right) Bob Tolan,
Pete Rose, Bench, and Alex
Johnson.

time the team had bestowed such an honor on
anyone.

Except for his earliest days in Tampa, Johnny
had always been confident; but all this success
and attention was causing him to become down-
right cocky. He began telling people, "Forget
Babe Ruth. Just remember Johnny Bench."

Before Bench could get too carried away with
dreams of glory, his 1966 season abruptly ended.
In the very first inning he caught for Buffalo, a
foul tip broke his thumb and the young star was
sent home to Oklahoma to recuperate. Unfortunately, his luck would get worse before it got
better.

In late August, Bench was involved in another serious accident when a drunk driver hit
his car almost head-on. Though Johnny suf-

fered a gash in his head that required nearly 20 stitches to close, doctors told him he was lucky to be alive.

Two near-fatal accidents in two years might have slowed a lesser player down. But Johnny Bench was not easily deterred. That fall, shaved head, stitches, and all, he was back in Florida, playing in the Instructional League again.

3
ROOKIE OF THE YEAR

Bench started the 1967 season as the regular catcher of the AAA Bisons. He did so well in Buffalo, hitting .259, but clouting 23 homers with 68 RBI's in 98 games, that he was named the Minor League Player of the Year. He did so well that before the season even ended, he was called up to the majors.

When reporters asked manager Dave Bristol about the Reds' call-up of their "prize rookie," Bristol said, "We're going to nurse him along slowly and patiently. Heck, he's just a kid."

Eager to see what the 19-year-old future star could do, the Reds started him against the Philadelphia Phillies on August 29th. And in his big-league debut at old Crosley Field, Bench did not do much. He went 0-3 as the Reds bowed to the Phillies, 3-2.

Nevertheless, Bench was back for the second

Bench's arm was feared by opposing base runners. From 1975 through 1979 the opposing team stole less than one base every two games in which Bench started, the best mark of any starting catcher.

game of the Phillies series and then the third, which he helped the Reds win 2-1 with his first major-league hit and his first major-league RBI. On September 1st, the San Francisco Giants came to town and Bench's name appeared on the lineup card for the fourth straight time. It was apparent that, despite manager Bristol's earlier words of caution, Johnny Bench was already the Cincinnati Reds' first-string catcher.

Naturally the Reds' veteran catchers did not like losing their jobs to the youngster, and they gave Bench the cold shoulder. Bench accepted their resentment as part of the price he had to pay for his own opportunity to make good. And the young rookie was definitely making good.

In the opener with San Francisco, Bench took a giant step in locking up the starting catcher's job. On the mound for the Giants was a very tough lefthander named Mike McCormick, who had already racked up 18 victories in 1967. The game was tied 1-1 when Reds first baseman Lee May led off the bottom of the seventh with a double. McCormick then intentionally walked second baseman Tommy Helms so that he could pitch to Cincinnati's rookie catcher. This was Bench's most important at-bat so far, and everyone was waiting to see how he would react to the pressure.

They did not have long to wait. After taking the first pitch for a ball, Bench calmly lined the next one all the way to the wall in left center field for a standup double that scored two runs and gave the Reds a 3-1 victory.

Bench continued to catch almost every game for the Reds. On September 21st, in a 9-4 win over the Atlanta Braves, he hit his first home run as a big leaguer. Although he still was not hitting for a very high average, defensively he was already playing like a seasoned pro. It looked as if nothing but an injury could force Johnny Bench out of the lineup. Sure enough, nine days later a foul tip split his right thumb and ended his season.

As it turned out, the injury was not entirely a bad break. When it occurred, Bench had not yet accumulated enough at-bats to qualify as a rookie for the 1967 season. That meant he would have all of 1968 to prove himself worthy of the National League's Rookie of the Year award. That was the goal that the young catcher set for himself.

After gaining some more experience playing winter ball in Puerto Rico, Bench was looking forward to the start of the 1968 season. Predicting he would win the Rookie of the Year award, he set goals for himself of a .260-.270 batting average, 15 home runs, and 80 RBI's.

Much to Bench's disappointment, the Reds decided to start the season with veteran Don Pavletich behind the plate. In the fifth game, however, Pavletich pulled a leg muscle, and Bench was brought in to replace him. That was it for Pavletich—he never caught another game for Cincinnati. Bench went on to catch 154 (out of 158) games that season, a record for a rookie. And at the plate he equaled or bettered his goals in each department with a .275 average, 15 homers, and 82 RBI's. Along with being named to the All-Star team, he won his first of 10 straight Gold Glove awards. And to top it all off, he lived up to his boast by winning the National League Rookie of the Year award, just edging out the Mets' Jerry Koosman. Bench became the first catcher ever to win rookie honors.

Baltimore star Brooks Robinson tries to score from second base but is tagged out by Bench in the third inning of game 4 in the 1970 World Series.

Although Bench's offensive statistics were outstanding for a rookie, the experts were even more impressed with his catching and maturity. Bench had tremendous poise and absolute self-confidence, which he called "inner conceit." He believed that providing leadership was an essential part of his job as the team's catcher. Right from the start he boldly took charge of things on the field. He moved fielders who were out of position, played his own position aggressively, fired the ball to any base at any time, and handled the pitching staff firmly.

Bench also showed that he was his own man, unafraid to be different or to try something new. Wearing a helmet while catching and using a hinged catcher's mitt instead of the old pillow-type mitt were two Johnny Bench innovations. And though Bench did not invent the one-handed catching style, he did popularize it.

But it was the young catcher's powerful throwing arm that amazed teammates and opponents alike. Describing the unbelievable strength of Bench's throws to second base, Reds shortstop Woody Woodward said, "You see the ball is coming so low, and you are sure you are going to have to one-hop it. But it keeps right on coming, never more than two feet off the ground, and it explodes on you."

For years the Los Angeles Dodgers had been terrorizing the Reds with their base-stealing, but Johnny completely shut down their running attack by throwing out three Dodgers in one inning the first time he faced them. Never again would the Dodgers—or any other team— run wild against the Reds with Bench behind the plate. Opposing players around the league quickly discovered that Bench was a master at blocking home plate and tagging runners with the kind of sweep tag that previously only infielders had used.

As good as he was, however, Bench still had room for improvement, especially when it came to catching outside pitches in the dirt. But veteran observers had seen enough by the end of Bench's first full season to say that he was already one of the best catchers in the major leagues and that he might wind up being the greatest catcher who ever played the game.

Bench's reputation was spreading quickly, even to the American League. Harry Dalton, an executive with the Baltimore Orioles, said, "Every time Bench throws, everybody in baseball drools." Over the winter the young catcher was the subject of several full-length stories in national magazines, and in spring training Ted Williams, the former Boston Red Sox batting star, gave him an autographed ball that said, "To Johnny Bench, a Hall of Famer for sure."

When the 1969 season began, Bench picked

up right where he left off the previous year, producing as a hitter and a catcher and constantly challenging the other Reds to follow his example. His leadership qualities were becoming so pronounced that his teammates nicknamed him "The Little General."

In a game against the Dodgers, Bench noticed that Cincinnati southpaw Gerry Arrigo was breaking off a good curveball but tossing a lazy fastball. To show the pitcher that giving less than a 100 percent effort was unacceptable, Bench reached out and caught Arrigo's fastball bare-handed! Both teams cracked up laughing, and the embarrassed Arrigo suddenly found his good fastball again.

The highlight of Bench's second full season

Bench tags out the Giants' Willie Mays at home plate. Led by Mays, Marichal, and McCovey, the Giants finished ahead of the third-place Reds in 1969, the first year of divisional play in the major leagues.

came in the All-Star Game, where he contributed a two-run homer to the National League's 9-3 victory.

Overall, Bench enjoyed a fine year, batting .293 with 26 homers and 90 RBI's, but still his team finished down in third place. Disappointed but not discouraged, the Reds had a "Wait until next year" attitude—and with good reason. Complementing Bench was a hard-hitting lineup that included Pete Rose, Bobby Tolan, Tony Perez, Lee May, and Tommy Helms. The Reds were never out of any ballgame, as they proved by winning one contest 19-17 and another 10-9 in 11 innings after trailing 9-0.

Because of the Reds' ferocious, consistent hitting during the summer of 1969, sportswriters had started calling the team "The Big Red Machine." The nickname stuck, and it would haunt Cincinnati's opponents for most of the coming decade.

4

PENNANT POWER

Johnny Bench holds five baseballs that spell out "N.L. MVP" after winning the National League's Most Valuable Player Award in 1970. He was named first on 22 of the 24 ballots cast.

When Bench reported to spring training in 1970, the Reds had a new manager named Sparky Anderson. Though the Reds were skeptical about Anderson's credentials—he had spent just one year in the majors as a good-fielding, but weak-hitting, second baseman—they were quickly won over by his infectious enthusiasm and constant encouragement.

With Sparky at the controls the Big Red Machine rolled over the opposition, winning 70 of the team's first 100 games. Near mid-season the Reds moved into the brand-new, artificially turfed Riverfront Stadium. In their last game at Crosley Field, Bench and Lee May gave their fans a memorable good-bye, hitting back-to-back eighth-inning homers to help the Reds beat the Giants 5-4.

The Reds kept on winning, finishing the season with a record of 102-60, tops in the Western Division, a whopping 14$\frac{1}{2}$ games ahead of the second-place Dodgers.

Several Reds turned in outstanding performances. But nobody else on the team, indeed nobody else in the league, had a season like Johnny Bench's. He had become the league's number-one power hitter, slamming 45 homers and knocking in an astonishing 148 runs—both record-shattering numbers for a catcher. Three of the homers came in a single game on July 26th against the St. Louis Cardinals and the great Steve Carlton. Nobody was surprised when Bench was named the league's Most Valuable Player; he was the youngest player ever to win the prestigious award.

After winning the Western Division with their hitting, the Reds used some fine pitching to sweep the Eastern champion Pittsburgh Pirates three games to none for their first pennant since 1961. Next came the Baltimore Orioles in the World Series. But even though the Reds scored first in every game except one, the talented Orioles blasted out 10 home runs (a record for a five-game Series) and won the Series 4-1.

Bench hit a homer of his own in game 2, but it was Baltimore third baseman Brooks Robinson who stole the show with excellent hitting and six spectacular defensive plays, including two diving stabs of line drives that robbed Bench of hits. Losing the Series hurt a lot, but the Cincinnati catcher later showed he had not lost his sense of humor. When Robinson was presented with a new automobile for being named Series MVP, Bench quipped, "If we'd have known he wanted a new car that badly, we'd have chipped in and bought him one."

Bench may have missed out on the car, but following his great season and World Series exposure he did receive all sorts of lucrative

Photography from the Lens of George Kalinsky

Johnny greets his father at the birthday party for his dad in 1971.

commercial and endorsement opportunities. Realizing his enormous value to the Reds, Bench also asked for a new three-year contract worth $500,000. When the Reds refused to give it to him he staged a brief holdout. Finally he settled for a raise that brought his 1971 salary up to $87,000, high pay in the days before free-agent bargaining, but considerably less than he had hoped for. Still, it was the half-million-dollar figure that staggered the public's imagination and caused Bench more than a little heartache the following season.

Bench's bat was really hot at the beginning of 1971. He hit .312 with 9 homers in April and collected his 100th career home run on May 17th. But after that he tailed off considerably, partly because of injuries to his hands and feet and partly because opposing pitchers had stopped giving him anything good to hit. Too impatient to take the bases on balls, he began swinging at bad pitches—and striking out. When the hometown fans decided that Bench was not earning his big salary and started booing him,

Sparky Anderson took over as manager of the Reds at the start of the 1970 season. In his nine seasons guiding The Big Red Machine his team finished lower than second place only once.

he tried even harder. But that only made things worse. He suffered a string of batting slumps, going 1-24, 1-22, and 0-20 on his way to a final average of .238. The team also played poorly, and the Reds wound up with a disappointing 79-83 record.

Bench's totals of 27 home runs and 61 RBI's would have been considered a good season's work for most players, but they represented too drastic a reduction from his previous year's performance to satisfy him—or the Cincinnati fans. After the glory and excitement of 1970, the 1971 season was a definite letdown.

That fall Bench returned once more to the Florida Instructional League to improve his hitting. At 23, the former National League MVP was already working hard on a comeback.

Meanwhile, back in Cincinnati, general manager Bob Howsam was pulling off a block-buster trade with the Houston Astros that instantly transformed the Reds from a good team into a great one. A total of eight players were swapped, but the key to the deal was Joe Morgan. The little second baseman would develop into a dangerous package of baseball dynamite, capable of beating the opposition with a great catch, a stolen base, or a home run. Along with Bench, Pete Rose, and Tony Perez, Morgan would lead the Reds to their greatest years.

Determined to produce a winner again, Sparky Anderson put the team through many long and strenuous workouts during spring training. None of the players minded, though; they were all aching to show the world that they were still The Big Red Machine of 1970 and not "the little red wagon," as one sportswriter dubbed them, of 1971.

The Reds, and Johnny Bench in particular, started off slowly in 1972. So slowly, that by the end of May the team was in third place behind the Astros and Dodgers, and Anderson was beginning to worry about losing his job. After dropping four games in a row to the Cardinals, the Reds were about to begin a long road trip when Anderson said to coach George Scherger, "George, if we don't turn it around quick, we ain't long for this place. They are going to boot us out of town."

The Reds desperately needed somebody to step forward and lead the team by example. Luckily, they had just the man for the job—the man behind the plate.

Starting on May 30th against Houston, Bench went on one of the greatest home-run sprees in baseball history. He homered in each of the next five games (all won by the Reds), hitting a total of seven round-trippers during the streak. Altogether he got 11 hits in 24 at-bats for a .458 average, drove in 13 runs, and scored eight runs himself.

Inspired by Bench's big bat, the other Cincinnati players started hitting, and soon the team was winning regularly. In the middle of June, the Reds captured first place, and at the end of the season they were once again on top of the Western Division, 10 1/2 games ahead of the Astros.

As for Bench, another spurt enabled him to close out the season in style. In a stretch of seven games he hit seven home runs to finish with 40 homers and 125 RBI's, both league-leading categories. The effort was good enough for Bench's second MVP award.

It was a great season for Johnny Bench, but

Bench's 1970 Topps baseball card.

he was not ready to celebrate yet. Though no one else knew it, Bench had reason to believe it might be his last. For in the first week of September he had received some frightening news. X-rays taken during a routine physical examination revealed a spot about the size of a half dollar on his right lung.

Was the spot a cancerous tumor? That question could be answered only by an operation that was scheduled to be performed after the season. It hardly seemed possible, but the strong young Reds catcher, apparently in perfect health, had finished the 1972 season and was heading into post-season play with the knowledge that he might be suffering from a life-threatening illness.

Once again, the Reds faced the Pirates in the N.L. playoffs. This time the teams split the first four games, and the Pirates were ahead 3-2 in the fifth and final game as Bench led off the bottom of the ninth inning. Three more outs and the Pirates would win the pennant.

Pittsburgh's ace reliever, Dave Guisti, worked the count to 1-2, then threw a sinker on the outside. Bench saw the pitch well and hit it hard to right field. The ball carried and disappeared over the wall for a home run to tie the score. The homer sent Riverfront Stadium into pandemonium and rattled not only Guisti but his replacement, Bob Moose, who five batters later wild-pitched the winning run home for the Reds.

After hitting one of the most important home runs in Cincinnati history, Bench was hoping to lead the team to victory in the World Series. The Oakland Athletics, however, had other ideas. Led by their own catcher, Gene Tenace, who stunned the Reds with two home runs in the

opening game and a total of four in the Series, the A's won three of the first four games. Although the Reds rallied to win the next two games, with Bench homering in game 6, they fell short, 3-2, in the deciding seventh game.

Despite the series disappointment, Bench was satisfied with the season because it proved that his great year in 1970 had not been a fluke. But while his teammates headed off for some well-earned rest and relaxation during the winter, Bench remained in Cincinnati, waiting for the operation that would determine his future.

Bench underwent his surgery on December 11, 1972, and the operation was successful. The spot on his lung proved to be nothing more than a benign fungus growth. Still, he experienced a lot of pain during his recuperation, which took several months, and the surgery left an ugly scar winding across his chest.

Bench always seemed to hit ninth-inning clutch home runs. Here he connects against the Pirates' Dave Giusti to tie the fifth playoff game in 1972. The Reds then won the game 4-3.

*After Bench slugged a
ninth-inning home run to
defeat the Mets 2-1 in the
1973 League Champion-
ship opener, he received a
congratulatory kiss from
his mother, Katy.*

Though few people noticed it, the surgery
hampered Bench's throwing motion and re-
duced his strength and quickness at bat—just a
fraction, but enough to affect his performance.
Under the circumstances, he did not consider
his 1973 output—25 home runs, 104 RBI's and
a .253 batting average—as disappointing as
some did. And despite his problems, there were
still plenty of days when he looked very much
like his old self. On May 9th, for example, he
again hit three home runs in a single game, good
for 7 RBI's, in a 9-7 win over Philadelphia.

The Reds defended their 1972 Western Division crown well at first, but in May the team's
weak pitching began to let them down. The Reds
just could not match the quality or depth of the

Dodgers' excellent pitching staff. Obtaining crafty lefthander Fred Norman from the San Diego Padres in mid-June helped some, but Cincinnati was still 10 games out of first place and presumed out of the running when the Dodgers came to town on June 30th for a four-game series.

The Dodgers won the opener and were one out away from winning the second game when third-string Reds catcher Hal King pinch-hit a three-run homer that gave Cincinnati a last-second 4-3 win. King's surprising clout seemed to turn the team's whole season around: The Reds won 60 of the last 86 games—and the division championship by 3½ games.

For the third time in Sparky Anderson's first four years with the Reds, the team was in the playoffs. Their opponents in 1973 were the New York Mets, who had struggled to the Eastern Division championship with a won-loss record (82-79) barely over .500. The Reds 99-63 record made the series look like a mismatch, and it was... except the Mets won.

Although the Reds stretched the series to its five-game limit, the superb Mets pitchers dominated play, limiting Cincinnati to 8 runs (5 of which came on solo homers) in 48 innings. Bench's bottom-of-the-ninth home run off Mets ace Tom Seaver gave Cincinnati a thrilling 2-1 win in game 1. But the big blast was small consolation when the Mets and not the Reds went off to play in the World Series. After this third straight post-season disappointment, Bench could not help wondering when, if ever, he would get to wear a World Series championship ring.

5

THE BIG RED MACHINE

It certainly would not be the next year; the 1974 Reds won 98 games, but the Dodgers, behind more great pitching and some excellent hitting by Steve Garvey and Jimmy Wynn, won 102. The Reds' slide from first place could hardly be blamed on Bench, however. He had one of the best all-around years of his career. In addition to winning his seventh consecutive Gold Glove award, he led the league in RBI's (for the third time) with 129 and was second in home runs with 33. He also ranked first in total bases and second in doubles and runs scored. If the Reds had finished in first place, Bench would most likely have won a third MVP award; as it was, he finished fourth in the voting.

By this time Johnny Bench was a major celebrity in Cincinnati. He had become friends with such national personalities as comedian Bob Hope, and the good-looking young catcher seemed to make as much news off the field as on

The 1975 World Series was one of the greatest ever played. Dwight Evans tries to score on a first-inning single by Fred Lynn and is tagged out at home plate.

it. When he married a New York model, Vicki Chesser, right before the start of spring training, the wedding was a major social event in Cincinnati.

But as he headed into the 1975 season, Bench was all business. He and the Reds were frustrated, certainly, but not disheartened. They knew they had a lot of outstanding talent, and they believed they were very close to putting it all together. Maybe this would be the year The Big Red Machine finally went all the way.

Johnny Bench could hardly believe his ears, but there was no mistaking the sound: On Opening Day 1975, some Cincinnati fans were already booing as his name was announced over the loudspeakers. Throughout the early part of the season the booing continued every time Johnny struck out or popped up. It may have been that the fans had unrealistic expectations of Bench. Whatever the reason for it, the booing disgusted Sparky Anderson, who said, "How a man could come to this club eight years ago and literally—I mean literally—put Cincinnati on the map, then get the treatment this man receives, is beyond me."

Bench, however, made no comment. He simply tried to ignore the crowds and concentrate on the game. Unfortunately, he soon had something more serious than booing to worry about. On April 22nd, in a fearsome homeplate collision with San Francisco's Gary Matthews, Bench tore the cartilage in his left shoulder. Although he received all sorts of treatment for the injury, it eventually became clear that nothing short of an operation was going to help. For the rest of the season Johnny Bench played and even slept in pain. Moreover, the injury robbed

The Giants' Gary Mathews slams into Bench in an April 22, 1975 game, knocking the durable catcher out of action.

him of his power to hit to left field. He immediately plunged into a 7-48 batting slump, his average dropping from .304 to .256.

Then, in September, Bench wound up on crutches for a few days after a Fred Norman pitch in the dirt bounced off his ankle and caused it to swell badly. The physical beating he had been taking for years became evident when doctors X-rayed the swollen ankle. Although they found no current breaks, they did find three old fractures in his foot that had never been detected. His injuries in 1975 limited Bench to 142 games, 121 as a catcher, his fewest so far on both counts. Nevertheless, he still got many clutch hits throughout the season and somehow

The Reds had a 12 1/2 game lead at the All-Star break in 1975. Five members of the rampaging Reds were selected for the National League squad: (left to right) Pete Rose, Bench, Joe Morgan, Tony Perez, Dave Concepcion. The bats in front show the number of times each player has been honored as an All-Star.

managed to finish with an impressive 28 homers, 110 RBI's, and a .283 average.

But even though Bench was not at his best, the Reds as a team were absolutely awesome in 1975. Sparky Anderson had found the final piece to the puzzle early in the year. On May 2nd the Reds were plodding along at 12-12 while the Dodgers were starting to build another lead. Before the game that night, Anderson noticed All-Star left fielder Pete Rose gobbling up grounders at third base during batting practice. Anderson realized that if he could get Rose to take over the third base position, which had so far been manned by several different weak-hitting journeymen, he could put a budding power hitter named George Foster in Pete's old spot in left. Suddenly Anderson found himself managing one of the greatest lineups in baseball history: Perez at first, Morgan at second, Dave Concepcion at shortstop, Rose at third, Ken

Griffey in right, Cesar Geronimo in center, Foster in left, and Bench behind the plate.

This most powerful model of The Big Red Machine started and then stalled a few times, but once it really got moving, it was almost unstoppable. The Reds made a joke out of the pennant race. By the All-Star break they were 12½ games out in front, and they finished with an incredible 20-game lead. They collected a total of 108 victories, the most by any National League club in 66 years, and were virtually unbeatable in Riverfront Stadium where they won 64 times in 81 games. And when they clinched the division title on September 7th, they set another record—for the earliest wrap-up in history.

This time the Reds blew away their old foes, the Pittsburgh Pirates, in three straight games to win the pennant. Even so, skeptics began predicting that the Reds would choke again in the World Series when they faced the Boston Red Sox.

The Reds did not choke against the formidable Sox, but they did not exactly sweep them either. In fact, the 1975 World Series was so closely contested that it produced five one-run games, five come-from-behind finishes, and two extra-inning contests. Boston won games 1, 4, and 6, while Cincinnati won games 2, 3, 5—plus the all-important game 7. Appropriately, the Reds' winning run in the rubber game came in the 9th inning. The 1975 championship was so hard-fought and so full of great plays and performances, constant lead changes and momentum swings, that most observers declared it a classic World Series, perhaps the best ever played for its overall drama.

Riverfront Stadium, home of the Cincinnati Reds. The first game played there was on June 8, 1970. Prior to that, the Reds, the oldest professional team in baseball, played at Crosley Field, which, under various names, was home to the team for 85 seasons.

There was at least one new hero every game, sometimes more. And even though he was injured, sick with the flu, and upset over his marriage, which was already heading toward divorce, Johnny Bench had his great moments as well, including a home run in game 3.

But Bench's best shot came in the top of the ninth of game 2 with the Reds trailing 2-1. Cincinnati had been shut out in the opener, which meant that their grand total for the first 17 innings of Series play was but one run. As Bench came up to lead off the inning, he noticed the Boston defense had swung around to the left in an effort to neutralize his power. With his bad shoulder Bench considered bunting, but instead he slapped Bill Lee's first pitch into right field and hustled into second with a double. Two outs later, Dave Concepcion's single drove Bench in to tie the score. Ken Griffey then doubled Concepcion home with the go-ahead run. In the bottom of the inning Rawley Eastwick retired the Sox in order—and the Cincinnati Reds were on their way to the world championship.

The Reds' World Series victory, their first in 35 years, sent the city of Cincinnati into a frenzy. And even though the personal problems that had plagued him during the Series made the triumph a bittersweet one for Johnny Bench, he celebrated with his teammates and shared their joy. For he was an integral part of a great team that had finally proven itself. As he said in the rocking Reds clubhouse after the big win: "We've been saying for three years we have the best team in baseball. Now it's really something, knowing that tomorrow we'll wake up and can say for the next few months that we're the champions."

6

THE SUPER SERIES

An operation in the fall of 1975 repaired Bench's injured shoulder. And as the start of the 1976 season rolled around, he looked forward to playing without injuries again. But suddenly muscle spasms in his back began causing him pain every time he swung a bat or threw a ball. No one was able to figure out what was causing the pain, and Bench suffered through it for the first five months of the season.

Not surprisingly, the ailing catcher's performance suffered too. He hit only 16 home runs, while his batting average fell to .234, his lowest ever in the major leagues. Things got so bad that some unsympathetic newspaper reporters even began writing that the great Johnny Bench was all washed up.

Fortunately, the powerful Reds were able to carry Bench during 1976, just as he had carried the team so many times before. Joe Morgan was then in the process of winning his second consecutive MVP award; George Foster was blossoming into the National League's RBI champ, and the Reds as a team would lead the league in

Against the Yankees' Ed Figueroa in game 4 of the 1976 World Series, Bench cracks a two-run homer to break a 1-1 tie.

49

home runs (141) and batting average (.280). Again, The Big Red Machine led the pack from May 30th on, coasting in 10 games ahead of the second-place Dodgers with a 102-60 record.

Although the Reds got along without a healthy Johnny Bench during the regular season, they were happy to find they would not have to do so in the post-season. Reds trainer Larry Starr finally figured out that Bench was likely suffering from a salt deficiency because he sweated so profusely, especially on hot days. So in early September the catcher began taking salt tablets, and as if by magic the mysterious muscle spasms disappeared. Bench continued to struggle at the plate for a while, but with the help of batting coach Ted Kluszewski, he regained his stroke just before the playoffs began.

The Reds would need all the talent they had against their Eastern Division rivals, a strong Philadelphia team that had won 101 games during the season. Experts predicted a close series, but the Phils never had a chance. Cincinnati was still a hungry ballclub with something important to prove. The Reds knew they would have to repeat as world champions before they would be recognized as one of the greatest baseball teams in history, and they would be satisfied with nothing less than such recognition.

As soon as the playoffs opened in Philadelphia, it was clear that the Reds were a team with a mission. They easily won the first two games, 6-3 and 6-2. And back in Cincinnati, they swept the series by scoring three runs in the bottom of the ninth, the first two coming on homers by George Foster and a rejuvenated Johnny Bench. Bench's clutch homer set the stage for what can only be described as "Johnny Bench's World Series."

Opposing the Reds were the New York Yankees, who had some big hitters of their own. But it was the base-stealing of the first two men in the order, Mickey Rivers and Roy White, that made their offense go. Until they came up against the best arm on any catcher in baseball, that is.

In game 1, Bench fired off two throws, one on a pick-off play to third and another on an attempted theft of second, and suddenly the New York speedsters were stuck in neutral. Rivers did steal one base in game 4, but only because the attempt, coming with the Yankees behind by two runs, caught Bench by surprise. Amazingly, nobody had stolen a base against him in 23 straight post-season games until then. In the 37 post-season games that Bench played through 1976, the opposition stole a total of only three bases against him. By comparison,

Bench dives into the stands at Yankee Stadium in an attempt to catch a foul fly. The Reds swept the Yankees in four straight games in the 1976 Series.

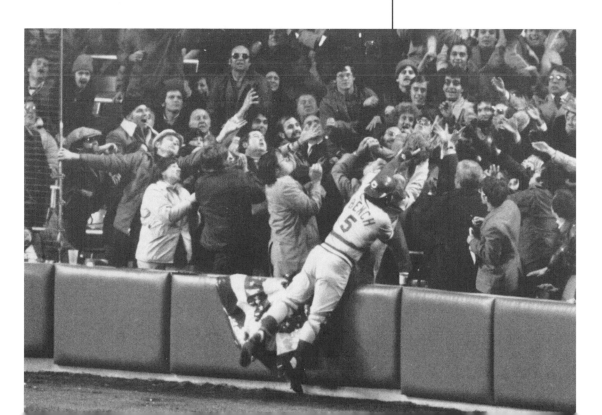

the Reds stole 50 bases against rival catchers in the same 37 games. And though he was not very fast, Bench accounted for six of those steals.

While Bench's arm intimidated the Yankees, it was his bat that destroyed them. He singled and tripled in game 1, singled and doubled in game 2, and singled twice in game 3. And then, in game 4, he smashed two homers as the Reds pulled off another sweep. That made them the first team in baseball history to go undefeated in both the playoffs and the World Series. For the Series, Bench batted .533 and led in RBI's with 6, which made him the only possible choice for the Series MVP award.

The stunning double-sweep made believers out of just about everyone. And when Joe Morgan asked, "How can you have a much better team than this one?" no one had an answer.

Similarly, people were wondering how any other catcher could possibly be as good as Bench. In the press box, baseball writer Roger Kahn marveled at Bench's talent. "He's the best I've ever seen," Kahn said. "But I only go back to Berra and Campanella," he added, referring to two great catchers from the 1940s and '50s. Red Smith, another great sportswriter and somewhat older than Kahn, then said, "He's the best *I've* ever seen, and I go back to Dickey and Cochrane [two stars from the 1920s and 1930s]."

But the highest praise came from the man who knew Bench best, Sparky Anderson. At the post-Series news conference a reporter asked the manager how he thought Thurman Munson, the Yankees' fine catcher, compared to Bench. Anderson said, "Don't embarrass nobody by comparing them to Johnny Bench." Munson, a gruff and proud man who had also performed

The Commonwealth of Grenada honored Bench in 1988 by issuing an official stamp with his picture on it.

outstandingly in the Series, was highly insulted by the comment, but Anderson had not meant to put him down. The jubilant Cincinnati manager was simply trying to say that Johnny Bench was the best baseball player he had ever seen. And after the 1976 World Series, a lot of people had to agree with him.

After the glorious peak it reached in 1976, The Big Red Machine rolled quickly downhill in 1977, but no one could blame Johnny Bench for the decline.

Between seasons, the Cincinnati management had made a big mistake by trading away popular first baseman Tony Perez. The team sorely missed his offensive production in the clutch as well as his ability to create harmony in the clubhouse. The loss of Perez combined with the third-highest earned run average among N.L. pitching staffs doomed the Reds to a second-place finish and wasted excellent efforts by George Foster (the league MVP) and Bench, who won his tenth and final Gold Glove award while batting .275 with 31 homers and 109 RBI's.

7

MILESTONES AND HONORS

The Reds won a few more games in 1978, but again they finished second. The Reds came roaring back in 1979 to win their sixth division title of the decade. Their opponents were the Pittsburgh Pirates, but this time the Pirates swept the three-game series.

What hurt the Reds more than anything else was the loss of key players who left the team seeking higher salaries than the Reds were willing to pay. Pete Rose was the first to go, after the 1978 season. And by the end of 1981, Morgan, Geronimo, Foster, and Griffey had all departed, too. Except for shortstop Dave Concepcion, Bench was the only member of The Big Red Machine's starting eight who seemed content to finish out his career in Cincinnati.

As one decade closed and a new one began, the extent to which Bench had contributed to the Reds became clearer than ever in the many

Bench is greeted by Hall of Fame catcher Yogi Berra. Berra held the record for most home runs by a catcher until Bench broke it with 314 home runs.

milestones he reached. On August 22, 1979, he clubbed a long home run against the Montreal Expos for his 15th of the season and the 325th of his career. With that homer he passed Frank Robinson to become the Reds' all-time home run leader. After the game Johnny spoke with reporters. "To become a home run king was all I ever wanted to do," he said. "What I've accomplished doesn't make me a Ruth, or Aaron, or even a Maris. But I'm still proud of it—very proud." By the end of the season he had something else to be proud of as well: a grand total of 1,013 RBI's for the decade, more than any other player in either league.

On July 15th he had hit yet another milestone home run, his 314th as a catcher, which broke Yogi Berra's record and made Bench the all-time home run hero at that position. When reporters asked him how he rated that homer compared to his other accomplishments, Bench said, "It's hard to top MVP awards. You can't put a price on them. For one swing of the bat, though, this can't be topped."

That year Bench caught over 100 games, for the 13th consecutive and final time. His total of 1,731 games caught placed him fourth on the all-time list. But catching so many games had taken its toll on him physically, and he told the Reds he could no longer be the team's regular catcher.

Bench wanted to play first base instead, but the Reds already had someone at that position— veteran Dan Driessen. When Driessen suffered a hand injury on May 2nd, however, Bench got his chance. But then, less than a month later, while hitting at a .343 clip, he broke his ankle sliding into second base and was out most of the season.

Bench played mostly third base during his last two seasons, 1982 and 1983. Because he was no longer as quick as he used to be, his performance there was merely adequate. The Reds as a team fared even worse, finishing far behind both years. Realizing that his best days were now behind him, Bench decided that 1983 would be his last season.

As soon as Johnny Bench announced his retirement, teams around the league began planning special days to honor him. Bench received lavish gifts from the rival teams, and, for the first time, the opposing fans chanted his name and cheered him. In Philadelphia he was applauded for hitting a three-run pinch-hit homer to beat the home team. The farewell tour was a very emotional experience, surpassed only by that magic September night at Riverfront Stadium when Johnny said good-bye to the hometown crowd with his last, dramatic home run.

Even in retirement Bench continued to live in Cincinnati and to maintain close ties to baseball. The Reds retired his uniform number (5) in 1984, and in 1987 he was hired to broadcast the Reds games for a local television station.

The ultimate honor came in 1989, however, when he was elected on the first ballot to the National Baseball Hall of Fame in Cooperstown, New York. Only Ty Cobb and Hank Aaron had ever received a higher percentage of votes than Bench did. The near-unanimous vote proved that although he spent his whole career in the National League, Johnny Bench was truly in a league of his own.

CHRONOLOGY

Dec. 7,	1947	Born in Oklahoma City, Oklahoma
	1965	Signs with Cincinnati Reds
	1966	Named Player of the Year in Carolina League
	1967	Voted Minor League Player of the Year
	1968	Wins National League Rookie of the Year award
	1969	Homers in first All-Star Game at-bat
	1970	Wins National League Most Valuable Player award
	1972	Wins second National League MVP award
	1972	Leads Reds to pennant with clutch homer in last game of playoffs
	1974	Leads National League in RBI's for third time
	1976	Voted World Series MVP
	1977	Wins tenth consecutive Gold Glove award as best defensive catcher
July 26,	1978	Hits home run #300
July 15,	1979	Hits his 314th homer as a catcher to become all-time home run king among catchers
Aug. 22,	1979	Becomes Reds all-time home run king with #325
	1979	Leads the major leagues in RBI's for the decade with 1,013
May 29,	1980	Hits three home runs in one game for third time in career
May 4,	1983	Singles for career hit #2,000
Sept. 17,	1983	Hits last homer of career on Johnny Bench Night at Riverfront Stadium
	1984	Uniform number (5) retired by Reds
	1986	Elected to Reds Hall of Fame
	1987	Becomes TV broadcaster for Reds
Dec. 19,	1987	Marries Laura Cwikowski
	1989	Elected to the National Baseball Hall of Fame
Dec. 17,	1989	Robert Binger Bench is born

(opposite page) Bench celebrates after hitting a home run on "Johnny Bench Night."

JOHNNY LEE BENCH
CINCINNATI, N.L., 1967-1983

REDEFINED STANDARDS BY WHICH CATCHERS ARE
MEASURED DURING 17 SEASONS WITH "BIG RED MACHINE".
CONTROLLED GAME ON BOTH SIDES OF PLATE WITH
HIS HITTING (389 HOMERS-RECORD 327 AS A CATCHER,
1,376 RBI'S), THROWING OUT OPPOSING BASE RUNNERS,
CALLING PITCHES AND BLOCKING HOME PLATE. N.L.
MVP, 1970 AND 1972. WON 10 GOLD GLOVES. LAST GAME,
9TH INNING HOMER LED TO 1972 PENNANT.

MAJOR LEAGUE STATISTICS

CINCINNATI REDS

YEAR	TEAM	G	AB	R	H	2B	3B	HR	RBI	BA	SB
1967	Cin N	26	86	7	14	3	1	1	6	.163	0
1968		154	564	82	155	40	2	15	67	.275	1
1969		148	532	90	156	23	1	26	90	.293	6
1970		158	605	97	177	35	4	45	148	.293	5
1971		149	562	80	134	19	2	27	61	.238	2
1972		147	538	87	145	22	2	40	125	.270	6
1973		152	557	83	141	17	3	25	104	.253	4
1974		160	621	108	174	38	2	33	129	.280	5
1975		142	530	83	150	39	1	28	110	.283	11
1976		135	465	62	109	24	1	16	74	.234	13
1977		142	494	67	136	34	2	31	109	.275	2
1978		120	393	52	102	17	1	23	73	.260	4
1979		130	464	73	128	19	0	22	80	.276	4
1980		114	360	52	90	12	0	24	68	.250	4
1981		52	178	14	55	8	0	8	25	.309	0
1982		119	399	44	103	16	0	13	38	.258	1
1983		110	310	32	79	15	2	12	54	.255	0
Total		2158	7658	1091	2048	381	24	389	1376	.267	68
League Championship Series (Total)		22	83	11	21	4	2	5	6	.253	4
World Series (Total)		23	86	16	24	4	1	5	14	.279	2
All Star Games (Total)		12	28	5	10	0	0	3	6	.393	0

FURTHER READING

Bench, Johnny. *From Behind the Plate.* Englewood Cliffs, NJ: Prentice-Hall, 1972.

Bench, Johnny, and William Brashler. *Catch You Later: The Autobiography of Johnny Bench.* New York: Harper & Row, 1979.

Blount, Roy, Jr. "Big Zinger From Binger." *Sports Illustrated*, XXX (March 31, 1969).

Devaney, John. "Johnny Bench: A Future Without Limits." *Sport*, XLVIII (December 1969).

Hertzel, Bob. *The Big Red Machine.* Englewood Cliffs, NJ: Prentice-Hall, 1976.

Kahn, Roger. "The Great J.B." *A Season in the Sun.* New York, Harper & Row, 1977.

Ratliff, Harold V. "Johnny Bench: Prodigy Behind the Plate." *Reader's Digest*, CII (June 1973).

Vecsey, George. "Johnny Bench, the Man Behind the Mask." *Sport*, LIV (October 1972).

Verdi, Bob. "No Gripes or Regrets for Retiring Johnny Bench." *Baseball Digest*, XLII (September 1983).

Wheeler, Lonnie, and John Baskin. *The Cincinnati Game.* Wilmington, Ohio: Orange Frazer Press, 1988.

INDEX

PICTURE CREDITS

Cincinnati Reds: pp. 2, 11, 19, 34, 46; Photography from the Lens of George Kalinsky, Major League Graphics: pp. 14, 17, 33; National Baseball Library, Cooperstown, NY: p. 60; Philatelic International: p. 52; W. F. Schildman, pp. 8, 58; Copyright the Topps Company, Inc.: p. 35; UPI/Bettmann Newsphotos: pp. 12, 20, 22, 26, 28, 30, 37, 38, 40, 43, 44, 48, 51, 54

The Major League Baseball trademarks depicted on page 52 are reproduced with permission from Major League Baseball Properties.

MIKE SHANNON is the editor and publisher of *Spitball, the Literary Baseball Magazine* and the author of *Diamond Classics: Essays on 100 of the Best Baseball Books Ever Published.* He has also edited *The Best of Spitball* anthology and written three chapbooks of baseball poetry. Born in Wilmington, North Carolina, and raised in Jacksonville, Florida, he is a graduate of N.C. Wesleyan College and Xavier (OH) University. He lives in Cincinnati, Ohio, with his wife Kathleen Dermody Shannon and their children Meghann, Casey, Mickey, Babe, and Nolan Ryan.

JIM MURRAY, veteran sports columnist of the *Los Angeles Times*, is one of America's most acclaimed writers. He has been named "America's Best Sportswriter" by the National Association of Sportscasters and Sportswriters 14 times, was awarded the Red Smith Award, and was twice winner of the National Headliner Award. In addition, he was awarded the J. G. Taylor Spink Award in 1987 for "meritorious contributions to baseball writing." With this award came his 1988 induction into the National Baseball Hall of Fame in Cooperstown, New York.

EARL WEAVER is the winningest manager in Baltimore Orioles history by a wide margin. He compiled 1,480 victories in his 17 years at the helm. After managing eight different minor league teams, he was given the chance to lead the Orioles in 1968. Under his leadership the Orioles finished lower than second place in the American League East only four times in 17 years. One of only 12 managers in big league history to have managed in four or more World Series, Earl was named Manager of the Year in 1979. The popular Weaver had his number 5 retired in 1982, joining Brooks Robinson, Frank Robinson, and Jim Palmer, whose numbers were retired previously. Earl Weaver continues his association with the professional baseball scene by writing, broadcasting, and coaching.